A *Romance* with the *Moon*

Carolyn Plesa

PublishAmerica
Baltimore

ISBN: 1-60441-405-7
PUBLISHED BY PUBLISHAMERICA, LLLP
www.publishamerica.com
Baltimore

Printed in the United States of America

ACKNOWLEDGMENTS

My sincere gratitude goes out to all who helped make this book possible.

I would first like to thank my cousin Richard Klein. The first person to look over my poems and say "I think these are really good". And my other cousin, Linda Klein Means, who said, "these are very, very good; yes, you have a book here."

I would also like to thank my close friends, William Birkett, Kevyn Kerdklotz, Kirsten Talko, Andrea Williams, and Elaine Brubaker. Who, although I drive crazy sometimes, have loved me unconditionally for over fifteen years.

There are a few more new friends that need to be mentioned. One is Lauren Smith, a new friend who liked my work and sent me in the right direction for publication. I would also like to mention Gail Novak and Julie, two new friends who have been extremely kind.

I will forever be grateful to these friends and family. Thank you all very, very much for your friendships and love.

Table of Contents

Chapter One
The Moon's Seasons

A CIRCULAR PATTERN

The Life of the moon
Creates a cycle of stages
A cycle of circular delights

As she waxes and wanes
Each month before our eyes
We watch her beginnings and her demise

Her circular purpose towards
Growth and dissemination
As her endings continue forward
To beginnings; the circle complete

These circular patterns in the heavens each night
Are for all to gaze upon in the evening light
As the story of the life of the moon burns bright

A HALF MOON

The moon is a thin slice hanging in the heavens
A single slant of brightness in an otherwise dim night
She is not even half full in her monthly process
The heavens made murkier without more of her light

Shared with her constant star companion
Presented under the moon's lower tip
Always there, always shining
This partner in the hours of the night

A star which is always more obvious
When the moon is not overly bright
When the moon is not quite half full
Not ablaze with light

Below this slanted fragile glow
The Venus Star shines with delight
Creating this special sight of the
Moon's monthly rite

When she is not quite half full
Not quite so big with light
The moon is marked by the blush
Of a star on it's lower right

A NIGHT OF STARS

There is no moon shinning tonight
The stars sparkle extra bright
As they wink between themselves
Their glow designs a neon light

As the stars sway back and forth
Across this dim massive scene
They dominate this evenings'
Sky with a play to be seen

Crisscrossing the heavens with
Their sheer light for this night
The stars might is revealed
On this evening's dark field

THE MOON IN SUMMER

The summer moon ascends into the sky
Before night begins, before dusk begins
And before the infamous twilight hour

As the sun lingers at the sky's border
The summer moon starts her journey
As the birds busy themselves before dark
The summer moon captures her position

Mixing with the sun's fading light, this moon
Transforms the shadows in the late afternoon
Her twilight glow highlights the garden flower
As the sky turns its many evening colors

At this special moment, before the stars appear
And the sun's rays dissipate
This summer moon hangs in the heavens
Radiating the peace and comfort of this day

THE MOON IN SPRING

Unlike my winter view of the moon
The Springtime Moon hides and escapes my eyes
Covered by the trees' leaves, she is high in the sky
Before I gaze into the night

But my body feels and my mind knows
The glorious full moon is present
I have missed her beginning and assent
She eludes me, this Springtime Moon

Unlike the Crone Moon which allows all to be seen
Brilliant with her radiance among the bare trees
She permits her splendor to shine brightly
As she passes unabated through the winter months

But as the seasons change, so must my moon
The Crone Moon passing by my window transforms
She alters herself, shielded by the new leaves on the trees
She is protected by the planet

Thus unobserved, this new Maiden Moon
Skips across the evening skies unnoticed
Until, unexpectedly caught unprotected
By the leaves on a tree, her light bursts

Across the heavens and into my room
My bedroom becomes fully lit by her blaze
This bold Virgin Springtime Moon shines
Through my window onto my bed

As she stirs me from my sleep
I smile and relax; it's only the Springtime Moon
Peeping into my room

THE SEPTEMBER MOON

The September moon, she calls to me
The September moon, she talks to me
She sings to me

She wants me to know the joys of our stories
The pains of our tales, the life within a life
The moon she calls, she calls

She wants me to know, she wants me to listen
The moon up in the sky
The moon of my life, she talks

She whispers in the evening breeze
Of our shared joys; of our shared pains
The moon; before our shared journey ends
Wants me to know, she wants me to understand

Her journey, my journey, our journey
The journey that continues for the moon
The circular journey of the moon

She wants me to know
She wants me to listen
She wants me to understand

That's why she calls to me
That's why she sings to me
That's what she wants me to know

And that's why I listen to the tales and to the stories
And that's why I can journey through the pains and the joys
And that's why the evening breeze and
The light from the moon calms my soul

THE CLOUDS

The clouds pass swiftly over the moon
Large snow drops fall from the clouds
Creating cloudy, snowy days and nights
Full continuous clouds pass in the evening
Pass over the moon which grows full each day
As it waxes and wanes behind the huge clouds

Over and over, and, over and over
Receding, reducing, expanding, filling
Over and over, and, over and over

The clouds pass over, the storms pass over
The snow keeps falling from the evening skies
Covering the land as the clouds cover the heavens
Thus, a thin veil of darkness hangs in the air
The moon's light only shadows on the clouds
Such a dark night fit only for a dream
A dream within the dream; within the dream
Held by the darkness and continuing
Into nothingness as it folds over within itself

Over and over, and, over and over
Expanding, filling, receding, reducing
Over and over, and, over and over

The passage of the moon is hidden in this winter's landscape
The full moon which should light up the nighttime sky
Is sheltered by the clouds, and the stars which should
Shine bright in the heavens are covered on this night
Thus creating a darkness more dark than usual
A darkness so complete, that the reality of the dream
Is magnified, and the dream within the dream
Is made more real by the starkness of this moonless winter night

Chapter Two
The Energy of the Moon

THE MOON

I stand alone with myself, alone by myself
To present myself, a dream, a dreamer, in this web of dreams
To the only constant, never ending light within
This dream; the moon

The moon which is destroyed within its rebirth
Over and over each month
It's constant light, its never ending presence
Gives me courage, gives me strength

Inflames my passions, my secret inner emotions
Stirs the ancient knowledge within my bones
Awakens old feelings within my sacred temple
And calls forth my primordial life-force

This moon, this moon
Draws me near
Draws me like a lover
Draws me to observe her monthly rebirth

Her monthly transformation up in the night sky
Carries me forward into my Crone side
Accepting the loss of my own monthly ritual
Her gifts move me forward into a new life

THE DANCE

The seasonal dance begins again
The dance of the earth begins again

So Come
Come dance with me, dance with me
Dance with me tonight

We'll dance upon the earth
We'll dance with the earth
We'll dance under the moon
We'll dance with the moon

So come
Come dance with me, dance with me
Dance with me tonight

As we dance, to the planet's cycle of seasons
We'll dance with the wind; we'll dance up into the wind
The wind will carry our dance of seasonal returns

So come
Come dance with me, dance with me
Dance with me tonight

The dance will carry us into the evening sky
We'll dance on the clouds we'll dance on the stars
We'll dance under the magic of the moon

So come
Come dance with me, dance with me
Dance with me tonight

Let's dance on the surface of the earth
Let's dance with the sounds of the wind
Let's dance under the light from the moon

We'll dance on the clouds we'll dance on the stars
We'll dance with the earth we'll dance with the moon
We'll dance the dance of seasonal returns

So come, come dance with me tonight

SUMMER SOLSTICE

The moon glides through the evening skies
Crossing through leaf-filled trees; she calls

All who will listen
All who feel her presence
All who will look upon her beauty

The peonies are blooming
The Dwarfs will come
The foxglove is blooming
The Fairies will come

The roses are blooming
The Elves will come
Some lilies are blooming
For the Special Ones

The yarrow is beginning to bloom
It will draw the Witches near
As we gather for a Summer Solstice Celebration
There will be song, merriment and dance

It will be a big assembly, a large festivity
For a special summer, a good summer
As we give thanks to the planet
And the gifts from our garden

Magic has been awakened and drawn near
As we honored the sun's warmth
And the beam from the moon

THE FLYING GEESE SONG

The many geese flying overhead singing their song,
Draws my attention to the heavens;
There hanging stately in the early evening is the moon

A half crescent moon glowing among the trees dark bare branches
A half crescent moon glowing amid the scattered, shifting clouds
A half crescent moon glowing & showing the wild geese flying by

Where does she come from to attract the seasonal energies?
When did she begin to lighten up the darkening heavens?
Why did she shine to herald the Sprites, long time forgotten?
How did she arrive to create magical magic twilight delight?

It's the moon, it's the moon that allows and welcomes
Earths hidden treasures to roam freely in her presence
These long time forgotten treasures can continue their work
In the light from the moon and the yearly song of the geese

The Sprites can begin playing upon the earth
Safe only in the moons company
They carry on, as she carries on
To perpetrate the existence of magic

As the Little One's dance
As the Elves sing
As the Fairies laugh
And as the Witches prepare
The moon shines

She provides the light for a long dance
A long song is sung to weave a long spell
For a final celebration to the year
The ritual to secure a place to sleep

To sleep for months, as the ground sleeps
As the flowers sleep and as the trees sleep
So shall the treasured Little Folks sleep
Safe in their protected hiding place

So they dance their dances, weaving in and out
Out and in, they dance among the sleepy plants
Gathering all as they weave their magic in the twilight

Only with the help from the moon
Only with the tipping of the planet
And only with the song of the geese

Can everyone know, can anyone sense
That it is time to pause, to rest, to sleep

WINTER BEFORE SPRING

In the dead of winter, in the undisturbed night
The full moon is vast and strong
The stars are sparkling and dazzling
The only activity in an otherwise serene scene

As night nears day, magic appears
As the light from the moon and the stars
Mix with the morning's early glow
The Little Folk awake from their sleep

Candlemas is here, the yearly observation
Of the tipping of the planet in the direction of the sun
Heading to rebirth, regeneration, to a jubilee
A resurrection is near, a party is to begin

Let the little people begin their jig
Let our spiritual souls start up and quicken to the steps
Let the movement of our bodily changes begin

As the little ones speed up their dance
And pull us from our sleep
The snow which blankets the earth melts
And the soil starts to warm up

As the special ones dance their dance
They harkin and carry Persephone near
As she rises to the planets surface
Far from Hades' icy grip, her soul warms
And she reopens to her mother

As the tepid dance tips emotions
It helps us speak our truth
Laugh at our follies
And submit to a new time

As the buds push forth
And the planet comes to life
A frozen soul turns warmhearted

THE HALF MOON

The half moon draws my attention
Hanging in the midst of the tree branches

Summoning spiritual, kindred
Souls to awaken

And look into the nights
Blessings given to all

DUSK

Look at the moon
She is up early this evening

Look at me, look at me, look up, please
See how I shine?
Look up, look up, look at me, please

I shine for you
I shine for all to see

At dusk, at the twilight hour
None in nature can compare
To a full moon rising in the air

Chapter Three
An Affair of the Heart

THE DANCE WITH THE MOON

Gazing upward to the evening sky
There in heaven hangs a magically
Half -empty, half- full crescent moon

This shape of the moon's monthly stage
Creates just enough light and just enough
Darkness for magic's delight

I tilt my face upward and send my energy outward
Thus my eyes may be blessed by the moons glory
My lips kissed by the moon's enchantment
And my face bathed by the moon's brightness

Ancient mystical energies swirl about in the evening winds
As the sacred hidden mysteries dance around me
My body is surrounded by the night's magical ritual

Slowly I begin to dance upon the earth's surface
The holy spiritual crescent moon dance
I surrender my body to my lover; the moon

Binding and blending the secrets of the heavens
The energies of the body, and the magic of the planet
I let go, release and dance the dance with my
New found partner, my new found lover, the crescent moon

A LOVE AFFAIR

A love affair with the moon
Three in the morning and I am
Wide awake, witness to the bright
Full moon filling the evening air

Like a lover, draws me near
Like a lover, always on my mind
Like a lover, a picture in my mind
Like a lover, I must be near

A fire of earthly essence
I ignite to attract your attention
Me, this earthly being is
Enthralled by your presence
Drawn by your brightness
Intrigued by your brilliance

MY LOVER

Come to me
Come to me from across the void
Sail through the cosmos, sail over the seas
Your light can be witnessed soaring in the heavens
Your burning beam can be easily seen
As you sail over the skies
And as you sail over the oceans, think of me
Let the thoughts of me urge you forward
Let the thought of me quicken your progress
As I wait for you

I calm my thoughts
I calm my actions
I calm my heart

How many times have we met?
How many moments have we experienced?
When will we connect again?
As we did last month
That one bright night, our first bright night
When we promised to meet again
As our hearts were joined together
And we pledged our souls as one
And now, as I seek and as I pray
For your speedy return

I long for your light's glow
I long for your feel
I long for your embrace

The touch to the body
The touch to the heart
The touch to the soul

So, sail to me my lover
Sail to me over hills and over stars
Come to me soon
As I lay waiting for you
As I lay waiting for your return

My body seeks
My heart longs
My soul prays
For the return of my lover's touch

SLEEPLESS NIGHTS

Awakened from my hollow sleep
The waning moon beckons
Through my bedroom window

Forced from my evening nap
She requests my company
This secret partner of the night

As I recognize her constant
Repeating presence in the skies
She allows slumber to return

THE TRUTH OF LOVE

The moon, my moon
Where is she?
I do not need to look far
She's always near in the sky
But, the secret miracle of the moon
Is as unreachable and unattainable
As the magic of the heavens

Not by demanding, not by wishing
Not by pleading, not by begging
Are these mysteries released

But like the moons many cycles & phases
Are revealed and understood
And as the universe's blessings and gifts
Are bestowed upon the land
The truth of the truth is learned by
Those who watch, wait, and believe

The warmth and puzzlement of the moon
Is unlocked for all to understand

THIS OLD MOON

It won't
Let go
This
Old moon
This love
This lover

Run away
Run far
Come close
Look into its face
Try as you might

It won't
Go away
It won't
Let loose
It will not permit
The bindings to be broke

Try to
It will not allow
To be let go
So, it's always there
This old moon

Try new tricks
Try new tales
There's no fooling
This old moon
This old love
That's always there

Chapter Four
It's About Life

THE STARS

The stars are bright in the sky
The half moon is low in the horizon

The Owl is talking in the tree
The cats are restless indoors

The leaves are dancing with the wind
I step outside my house to join in

PASSION

As my body and my mind open
To a new stream of consciousness
I turn myself towards a new light

I turn my physical form
I turn my psychic form
I turn my mystical form

As I slowly turn my face in a new direction
I can feel the rhythm and the energy
In my mind and in my body soar

This old body that seeks, that demands rebirth
This old body that aches for understanding
Allows this new energy to run wild

This force whispers in my mind
Of the ancient mystical knowledge
And knocks on my heart as I turn

Softly touching the shell of my heart
Softly touching again and again
Until the outer shell of my heart is shattered

Only then can my heart feel; can my heart accept
The new rhythm, the new energy
Traveling within my body and within my mind
Thus making my turn complete

THE WIND AND THE RAIN

The wind and the rain touch my face
These elements touch my body
The wind, the rain, the elements
Touch my face, touch my body

The mysteries and the blessings touch my soul
These elements of the cosmos touch my consciousness
The mysteries, the blessings, and the elements
Touch my soul, touch my consciousness

The knowledge and the wisdom touch my mind
These elements of the Crone touch my continuum
The knowledge, the wisdom, the elements, the blessings
Touch my mind, touch my body, and touch my continuum

These elements of my continuum justify my existence

GRANDMOTHERS

Oh my grandmothers come down
Join my heart, my soul, and my mind as one
Forever now as one

Oh my grandmothers, please come down
To make me complete
Forever now as one

THE WIND

The wind has stories
The wind tells stories

Does anyone listen?
Does anyone know?
The stories that are carried by the wind

Listen to the wind
There are always tales to be told
Pay attention as the leaves rustle
With the voice of the wind

Sometimes it is a sweet whisper
Telling a tale long time forgotten
Empty yourself and absorb this wisdom
The whisper is soft, but the knowledge is strong

It is a sound which is carrying the mysteries
Of the universe passing swiftly on it's course
The song of the wind fleeing through the leaves
Is connecting to your soul's purpose in the breeze

THE MAGNOLIA TREE

She said the Magnolia Tree was in bloom
When she brought me home,
The morning's air still sharp
That's right, a Midwestern spring
Right after the crocus paints the lawns
And the tulips pop through the soil

It was a difficult birth, a long labor of love
For the special baby; a baby girl, after two boys
She was happy and tired, but mostly worried
Worried about passing the sacred knowledge
The knowledge passed between women
About women, and only for women.

Did it begin with Eve, with Lilith?
Mary Magdalene, Ruth, or Sophia?
The names of women throughout history
Aphrodite, Shapiro, Helena of Troy and Cleopatra
There are many names

Is the knowledge passed through the genes?
Absorbed within the mother's milk?
Or by the stories told by the fire at night?
Maybe it's the long hugs or the special
Kiss on the forehead that fortells the struggle,
The struggle that can last a lifetime if you allow

Like a Willow Tree that bends in the wind
So is the life of a woman.
Like an old Oak Tree with many branches,
Supporting many branches,
So is the life of a woman.
And like the Magnolia Tree's
Spectacular fragrant blooms in springtime
So is the life of a woman.

Bend, she says, as you support and as
You allow your daughter to blossom

ANGEL

What kind of an angel watches over
A poor wretched soul like mine
What kind of an angel watches over me?

That sits on my shoulder
Unaffected by my sins
Silently observing the pain
Of a day in a sea of dreams

What angel witnesses the path of a
Soul's journey through the illusions
Like shotgun sounds in the evening
Splits reality

What kind of an angel watches over me?

THIS TIME FOR ME

Alone in my evening bliss
I am freed by my loneness
Left to discover my abilities
In this time for me

Left to listen to my heart in this time for me
Left to feel my passions in this time for me
Left to smell my fears in this time for me

Left to accept my talents, my skills, in this time for me
Left to witness my failures, my falsehoods in this time for me
Left to join together the pieces of the oneness of me
Only then can I move forward to the truth and begin to live
Mutually as one with my passions, my fears and my talents
And my constant companions, the moon and the stars

A TIME FOR ME

This time to myself; this time for me, is a lonely place to be
Bruised feelings and battered emotions collected throughout
A short life are no longer callus markings upon my skin
I am once again hurt and fragile, my body bleeding and crying
As I re-examine the pile of sentiment which is me
I become exposed and naked, damaged goods for all to see

Some come to heal me
Some come to heal themselves
Some come to hurt more
Some come to bear witness
Some come with compassion, some come with hate
Some come with wisdom, some come with ignorance

But all come
To this play, to this dream
Of this time for me

THE PLACE OF IN-BETWEEN

Where on this planet
Is the space of in-between?
Where during this quest
Is the place of in-between?

Of peace
Of surrender
Of truth

At every turn illusions face me
As I search for my place of in-between
As I turn, as I search, as I seek
The illusion is performed before my eyes
Why run? Why hide? Why pretend?
That the illusion does not exist
I close my eyes and scream
As the illusion plays out

If only the illusion was a dream
But, the body born feels
The body born hears
And the body born sees
And the body's soul aches, it aches
And it weeps and it weeps
As the dream is completed

On this lonely planet, at this lonely time
Searching and looking for the space
For the place of in-between
I'll meet you there
In this place of surrender, peace and truth
I'll meet you there someday

THE STONE

Like a new born, a smooth stone
Skips over the water, flying high
Moving swift it gracefully touched the water
Playfully skimming the top's surface

Then, no longer swift, no longer skimming the top waters
The stone plunges and sinks into the sea
Immersed, the water bombards the stone from all directions

That same stone, now bruised, now recreated, re-shaped by nature
Is forced by time, by movement, towards the sea's surface
No longer new, but marked by circumstances through its journey
The water still flows over and still touches the stone

Amused, the stone splashes and slides about at the sea's edge
Happy in her rebirth

Chapter Five
It's About the World

TRUTHS

So alive, so strong, so fragile
So knowing, so unknowing
So wrapped in emotion
Too complex to understand

A time of confusion
As you try to unravel truths
Too intricate to comprehend
Too astounding to believe

A time of trusting your instincts
And letting go of old beliefs
Releasing old knowledge
And grasping new paths

CHANGES

58

Emptiness is greatness

Empty your body
Empty your mind
Empty your heart
Empty your soul

Empty it all, so that transformation occurs

THE MORNING

As night becomes day in the
Early hours of this morning
Winter Solstice occurs as
The moon and the planet tips

Shaped like an egg, the moon
Hangs near an old Oak Tree
An owl calls from near by
Another answers from afar

I stand outside in the presence of nature
I have the owls, the trees and the moon
I have the shape of an egg hanging in the sky

Promising the newness of birth
In the still sharpness of a winter's
Night sliding into day

I have sunrises, that quiet moment
To one's self with the world

THE HEAVENS' DAYBREAK

The clouds in the morning sky
Are touched by the soft rays raising
From the below the earth's horizon

Altered by the unrisen sun, the clouds
Create a new image across the heavens
An array of color spreads out for all to see

Dull pink, light orange, soft purple
These rays change the scene before our eyes
Marking the morning clouds drifting by

The early sunrise shine replaces
The last evening's shallow dim glow
In this, the heaven's changing show

Bewildered and distracted as the sun's flame
Bursts before our eyes, we become mesmerized
Once again as we watch a new day rise

EARLY MORNING

The early morning moon
Is a slice of light
Hanging in the horizon

Such is life
A precious slice of love

THE SOUNDS OF GEESE FLYING

The sounds of geese flying overhead
Geese in flight and singing
Occurs twice yearly

Once as they arrive in springtime
Then again near the season of fall
The sound of geese flying fills the air

The geese's song tells me of things to come
An easy reminder of seasonal change
Just a short moment, just a short note

The sounds of wings, sounds of songs
Embodied in the geese, flying over, flying by
Foretell of a journey repeating

And as they fly over my house, above my window
I can only listen and wonder and marvel
At the magnificence of it all

PRETTY BIRDS

Pretty birds, pretty birds
Pretty birds up in the trees

Pretty birds, pretty birds
Speak to me

Let me hear of your travels over seas and over lands
From tree to tree, through winds and through clouds
Sing to me pretty birds, sing to me
It does not matter if I understand your song
It matters that you are singing and that I am listening

It is the moment that matters here

A HORSE

The wind was there, bold and strong
With mysteries to reveal
The clouds were there, passing swiftly
With pictures to present
The birds singing as they flew over head
To you, to me or to themselves, I wish I knew
The dogs and cats, always near, wanting to be seen and touched
Happy compassionate beings, easily exchanging thoughts

But, Oh, the horse, the big powerful and majestic horse
Not needing much, wanting not much, content with its existence
Willing to exchange emotions only if accepted or accepting
Shows its power at its leisure, at its bidding
Or nothing is disclosed
Not like the wind which yearns for you to listen
Not like the clouds or the birds in the sky
Which pass by with their secret gifts'
Not like the dogs and cats which demand your attention
And not like the moon which harkens your soul

No

The horse waits for acceptance
Feels for openness
Looks for consistency
Before displaying mysteries
Sharing mysteries or love

HOLLYHOCKS

Hollyhocks, say the word, let your lips smile
Hollyhocks, say the word, let your mind wonder
Hollyhocks, look at the colors, let your eyes explore

Like other flowers, orange, yellow, red and pink
Or are they that defined, blended by the suns haze
As they become a mixture of the summer suns rays
They are the colors of nature that drive artists to paint

Hollyhock, feel the texture of the stocks
Soft and delicate, like velvet
Yet strong, bold and healthy

Unlike other flowers climbing towards the sky
They stand alone without help, resourceful on their own
Hollyhocks, ancient, alive and true

DAWN

Before the birds begin their songs
As the thin dark branches outline the sky
There is a silence

An expectancy upon the earth
Like a moment before a birth
It's as if every living creature
Every living substance pauses

As the planet shifts, as the suns rays slip into view
Our world awakens to another day
The dark branches turn a bit darker
The sky a bit lighter

Thus the awakening begins
It is not a flash of brilliance
It is not a chorus of hallelujahs
It is gradual

It does not take your breath away
This inconspicuous continual event
Although it should
No; instead dawn gives breath to us all
And as it gives breathe to new beginnings

The birds sing
The sky colors
And all creatures big and small
Open their eyes to daybreak

A new day full of wonders
Full of new adventures and new dreams

DREAMS

Mirror to mirror
Dream to dream
Never look far to see thyself
Never look far to see others
Never look far for answers unanswered

Mirror to mirror
Dream to dream
Never seek far for new beginnings
Never seek far for additional dreams
Never seek far for blessings from above

Mirror to mirror
Dream to dream
Never wonder why, never ask why
Always remember; it's as it should be

Mirror to mirror
Dreamer to dreamer
Never stop dreaming

TIME

May father time kiss you sweetly
On the cheeks as he passes by

May mother earth wrap her arms around
Your heart and send my love your way

So may the winds of time
Travel smoothly through your life

Chapter Six
Abstractions

THE SPRING RAINS

Newly awaked from its long winter sleep
The planet thirsts for the spring rains
Sometimes soft and moisturizing
Sometimes hard and cleansing

But always wanted and needed
The spring rains are called
And as always with the yearly cycle
The requested rains are released

Given by the universe the rains are
Set free to the desires of the planet
Needing the cleansing, she endures the abrupt hard washing
Wanting the moisture, she seeks the gentle soft wetness

Once nourished, once fully awake and conscious of herself
The planet cautiously responds to the nurturing rains
She slowly frees herself from winter's icy grip
And is ready to allow growth upon the land

SUMMER

The sounds of summer
The stillness in the air
The completeness surrounding the land

Life has grown
The sights, smells and sounds confirm
The growth upon the soil

THE LIGHT OF PEACE

The light, it shines on me
Shines on my body, shines on my skin
Warms my heart, heats my soul

This light of peace, of love
Of hope and of joy
The universal light shines daily
On me, on you, from above

This light that shines
As we walk in the garden
That does not belong to us
Is a gift from beyond

Walk softly and try not to do harm
To what does not belong to you
In the garden of delight

Because as the earth aches, we ache
And as we cry, the heavens cry
And if the garden darkens
Our days will be shortened

So try not to disturb the light
Of hope, love, peace and joy
As you walk through on borrowed time

AWAKE

Once awake; awake
Once awake, you know
Everyone knows
The planet knows, people know
Plants know, animals know
The cosmos knows

Once awake; you know, you know
Once awake you know
Once aware, always aware of knowing
Of the knowledge of the presence of awakening
Of the knowing of the presence
The presence of knowing of the awareness

Once awake, always conscience of knowing
One is not allowed to be unaware
Not allowed to not be witness, to the presence
Once aware of the presence's play
The show is played for all who know
All who are awake, all who will witness
All who care

YOU

When you have nothing
You need nothing

When you are no one
No one needs you

When you need nothing
You are you

You get to be you!

UNPLUGGED

Get unplugged to the
Dharma, the samara, the delusions
    The body

Get plugged into the
Cosmos, the consciousness, the continuum
    The soul

CIRCLES

Is it about mistakes?
Is it about beginnings or endings?
Is it about circles that never end?

Does it really ever end?
Can we ever end the circles of distraction?
Ever end the universal continuum?
Must we wait for all to reach the sun's rays?

Oh; for something new, something different
To not always move in a circle
Something to move a soul from one spot
To another; from one eternity to another
Oh; to just move and not repeat

Oh; to just move and not repeat

WHY

Why, oh why ask why
All is as it is to be

MAGIC

Magic, magic everywhere
Magic, magic enter here

Let the magic guide you to forgive
The ones who have hurt you
So that you may forgive yourself

Through the magic of forgiveness
Love of yourself grows

Let the magic guide you to forgive
The ones who have hurt you
So that you may love them

For it is the magic of love
Which frees' the soul

Magic, magic everywhere
Magic, magic enter here

Magic is always around
Open your heart and soul

Magic will appear
And brighten the horizon

Magical moments are always
Around to embrace

Become aware, dance the dance
And gladden your heart to life's miracles